THE WALKING NERVE-ENDING

A collection of poems and reflections by
Maisha Kiana Perkins

To: Gail!
Thanks for
the support!
♡ Mau

ISBN-13: 978-0692174111 Mai Content LLC
ISBN-10: 0692174117

DEDICATION

*This book is dedicated to the memory of my grandmothers,
Georgia Mae and Betty Jean.*

One writes out of one thing only—one's own experience. Everything depends on how relentlessly one forces from this experience the last drop, sweet or bitter, it can possibly give.

~James Baldwin, "Autobiographical Notes," in the *Collected Essays* from Library of America

TABLE OF CONTENTS

PREFACE

May 30, 2017

During the late spring, I sat down one evening to watch the PBS special, *Maya Angelou: And Still I Rise.* While watching the documentary, I experienced a deeper understanding of Dr. Angelou than I'd felt since first reading her poems and memoirs as a girl. I've been well-acquainted with her words and stories all of my life, given the time I spent, like most brown girl poets, reading every autobiography and collection of her poetry I could get my hands on from the Los Angeles Public Library. So it was no surprise to learn that she had spent several years as a child refusing to speak. I won't go into the details of why Maya spent five years mute by choice. The documentary covers this at great length. But what did strike me in this instance were two things. The first was the vision and faith that young Marguerite's grandmother had in her ability to become a world-class orator, captivating audiences on just about every continent despite her momentary season (albeit, years!) of silence. It hit home. Reminded me of the faith and support that my parents have always had, and continue to have, in my ability and talent as a writer. This is, of course, despite the length of time it has taken me to complete and publish a first manuscript.

The second point that grabbed me, I'll let Maya

Angelou explain in her own words: "When I decided to speak, I had a lot to say." When. I. *Decided*.... The way she phrases, "when I decided to" resonates deeply within me. I have long been a poet, and have grown to become a thinking writer. When I finished my Masters of Fine Arts in Creative Writing from Sarah Lawrence over ten years ago, I had no real plan for when or how I would publish my books. I just wanted to become a better writer. I knew publishing would happen at some point, but I did not feel compelled or entirely ready to figure it out once I'd completed that program. (I had similar "What now??" experiences when I finished my degrees at Howard University while considering the Peace Corps, and later at The New School. Quite the trend. I like to think of it as the Malcolm Gladwell "Late Bloomers" effect, from a 2008 *New Yorker* piece in which he examines the phenomenon of talented, potential-laden creative types who reach their greatest achievements comparatively late in their journeys.)

So I kept living, experiencing life and the other adventures that would ultimately enhance my writing. And then ten years passed. In that time, I fell in and out of love, packed up my Brooklyn apartment for a beachfront property in the United Arab Emirates, returned to the States, and completed a second Masters that did not lead to a PhD. Bouncing around the globe, I touted myself a *bon vivant* relishing in life-changing growth, in essence: *Mai on the Move*! But, I still wasn't ready to complete a manuscript. A few poems here and there have made their way into anthologies. I've kept several blogs at different points and developed a readership. And I'm regularly invited to contribute to online publications. But, where was my book? *My* work? I have written and saved tons of my pieces in the last decade, sending poems and chapters and long letters to dear friends who cherish what merit or amusement they find deep between the lines. But, I am only now starting to feel ready. By "ready" I mean pulling several of my poems together into a collection to finally be published.

While I am still processing a lot of the experiences I've had since leaving Los Angeles, especially while living in the Middle East and Hong Kong (and other shenanigans in my beloved New York City), I realize that sometimes what you think needs to "get ready" is already done. When I finally sat down and pulled out a bunch of my old poems (and a couple of brand new ones), there were over fifty gems I had available for my first collection, *The Walking Nerve-Ending* (which shares the name of my MFA thesis). I already had the cover art, having asked my cousin-in-law to design it for me several years ago. I'd already edited and revised the bulk of the lines you will read in this collection several years ago. In fact, a good portion of the poems themselves were written as I met with my thesis advisor, the poet Tom Lux, at Sarah Lawrence. Several years ago! Maya had it in herself to speak during those traumatic years of silence, but also had her own reasons (completely valid unto herself) of why she would not

9

speak until she was ready. Likewise, I don't question why it has taken me so long to curate this selection of my words for an audience to take part in.

I simply defer to the truth, *my truth*: As I decide to put these poems and reflections together in my first book, it turns out, I have a lot to say.

My Grandma's Hands

Grandma's hands, boy, they really came in handy... ~Bill Withers[1]

My grandma's hands have a story to tell—
not about how they ache and swell,
but how they've guided her through life so well.

This life, well-planned according to the Master's hand,
has covered a multitude
and planted roots that began in her own backyard.

My grandma's hands have protected and touched
the lives of those who needed them most.
My grandma's hands were shields of comfort
when young'uns needed to be held close.

My grandma's hands are TOUGH.

Her hands have picked loads of cotton and loads of
laundry,
wiped little bottoms and smacked big mouths.
Popped hands, pressed hair, plucked splinters,
and burped everyone's babies.
These hands have written checks
that support individuals and families.

---

[1] Withers, Bill. *Just As I Am*. Sussex Records, 1971. CD.

My grandma's hands have clapped, they've praised;
Clapped and praised the Lord.
Clapped and praised the Lakers!

Her hands have flipped the television
from her sports to her stories
while circling every word in the search
as she eats her glazed doughnut.
I've seen these hands fry chicken and bake 7-Up cakes,
as she sips her morning lukewarm coffee
in the middle of the day.

My grandma's hands have taken weekend trips to Vegas
with high hopes of big earnings from the nickel slots.
She'll journey back East,
or Far East on a birthday cruise
with a few of her kin.

Her hands have nurtured many gardens
of collards and mustard greens,
red tomatoes, white daisies, roses pink;
Cultivating tirelessly—
picking, pruning, arranging
offspring into her prized bouquet,
to honor her life and celebrate her love.

This Song, It Holds Our Youth

It's easier to build strong children than to repair broken men.
~Frederick Douglass[2]

I look north to find hope, because north is where our
heart is.
I look north to find strength, formidable presence, united
in stance.
I look north to find our home, teaching the lessons we
learn through life.
I look north to find our peace; Kabala, our muse, is
breathing our song.

This song, it holds our history,
proven courage in early centuries.
A people of the Continent returned to shores
that the Province of Freedom provided for.

This song, it holds our beauty
reflecting sun on the Salala stream,
we climb atop mount Wara Wara,
and inhale Koinadugu's breathtaking scene.

This song, it holds our tragedy,
heavy memories, war-torn nobility,
brutal reality, dehumanized youth,

---

[2] "Frederick Douglass Quotes." BrainyQuote.com. Xplore Inc, 2011. 13 August
2011. https://www.brainyquote.com/quotes/frederick_douglass_201574

our world's displaced in search of truth.
This song has been our security,
a decade's conflict of civil war,
in the midst of losing loved ones, leaders,
our ability to sing has endured.

This song, it holds our nation,
Noir survivors, beloved land.
Youth, empowered, sing our message of peace,
on this world stage, together, we stand.

This song is our potential,
it represents our dream,
this song defines reality
and our future, beyond the gleam.
Our song provides the music,
a bridge toward abundant goals.
This song, our esteemed purpose,
is resounding strength within our soul.

*Written with love for the students of Kabala Secondary School,
Sierra Leone. 17 March 2011.*

Starfoods, NYC, 2:45 AM

friday night Freedom
revival of New Jack Swing
hip-hop's sanctuary
the house of House
and in I jump,
hips first—
past cliques of eyeballs and attitudes
anchored in the *boom* of the jam.
        I don't skim turbulence
searching thresholds for scooting in
but rather lively up my own
by way of uninhibited
rip-roar—

Karavas, West 4th @ Cornelia Street, NYC

Why not wear a kimono to the West African dance class? ~Nikita S. Adams

The only place
you're likely to find a couple
of Japanese lads, in the middle
of a Greek bar, break-
dancing to the *guajira son*,
"Guantanamera"
is hidden deep in the heart
of The Village—

I find my bliss
within this urbane mélange: an old song
arranged new.

Farquharson

Dreads, tucked
behind one ear,
boogie across
the span of his back.
Together, full lips embrace
a perfect sequence of teeth
while his eyes
grin and slant
with one-two-step concentration.
His skin developed
in Caribbean sunset,
a mosaic: Black
River sand meets
Hudson River shore.
The sweaty surface luring
indiscriminate caressing
by a collective of
frisky fingers
delighted to discern the effects
of full body training
beneath his ribbed tank.
6 foot 5 inches
of musculature.
Frame as broad
as his height.

Could've drove steel,
been an all-star
on the field or a backwoods
lumberjack. Possibly
a high sierra, redbone redwood,
positioned near the
entrance on 1st and
1st Avenue, swaying
to the beat.

Contemplation @ Sweet Rhythm, 7th Avenue South & Bleecker

fluorescent neons sway
from the blue-tiled ceiling
of Sweet Rhythm.
i'm lost
between a bessie smith moan
and some variant form of jazz fusion.
caught in a midnight daydream,
i swoon and plot tall ambition:
one day . . . is a garnish on our
buzzed heart-to-heart.

his question
makes a hot circuit around my mind:
      so what *do* you wanna be
      when you grow up . . . ?
he wants to know
four weeks and a few hours before
another year, my twenty-sixth, is set to begin.
i grin, contemplating.

      clair huxtable,
      but my dude will be better than cliff!
      I'm not a lawyer though, I need something
      flavorful—
      like the grande dame supreme of
      artistic ingenuity, historical integrity and
      musical splendor,

(what exactly that means, we sip and both wonder)
      where i can get a fix
      of live salsa or chips and salsa,
      some groovin' disco, a little roots-soca-kaiso-
      calypso,
      or gospel and blues when the spirit moves--
      a place where my comrades and i have a stage
      to call home;
      desk, laptop and
      a hammock in a room,
      my favorite pen, some gin,
      and a view of the moon.

      and he won't be a doctor—
      but a curator of fly renaissance,
      producing exhibitions, plays, or playing gigs
      throughout the world
      or at our private digs.
      a sapioromantic, cerebral kind of love
      dynamic and driven, not afraid of commitment
      with dreamy eyes, soft lips and a big
      . . . available balance.
i chuckle, he blinks. we take a long sip of the moment.

      surely i'll be mommy
      at some point, i suppose,
      expanding the mind of my little one,
      or the minds, if it's in the design, of my little tribe.
      family field trips to the schomburg
      for talks on tuesdays,
      brighton beach wednesdays,
      summerstage saturdays,

shakespeare in the park every thursday.
catch the wiz under the stars
on the last friday in august,
to the house of the Lord on sunday afternoons;
sleep in, of course, on mondays in june.
take holiday excursions in the winter or fall;
after all, we'll have to make time to be enthralled
by the other six continents . . .

   damn!
he says,
      i'm in love . . .

Fuego en el tren

almost/siamese
they sit connected
by head-
   phones blaring daddy yankee
or some other *borinqueño*
delegate of *el reggaetón* massive

and it's in
overhearing
   the sensual blend
of dancehall *y bomba*
that i realize how
embarrassingly
attracted i am
to you
   if i could
lean in just/close/enough
to feel your
fuego—

The Zampoughi

Lilly done the Zampoughi every time I pulled her coattail...
~Melvin Van Peebles[3]

...like the hips of sista' Lilly
swangin' the *ZAM-PA'OOO-GEE*,
she winds & ticks
her essence, exposed to the beat.
six/eight stimulates the nerves
within her squared elbows,
heavy shoulders,
those ready thighs.
her feet mimic
the music in her eyes.

brothas & others
—spellbound—
wanting to get funked by her,
yearn to wrap both hands
around her succulent moves;

her electric motion
unbearably magnetic
to their touch.

they witness her twirl

---

[3] Van Peeples, Melvin. *Brer Soul*, A&M Records, 1968. CD.

into gyration, her vibration:

>   *cocoa pop! watch me*
>   *shimmy-shimmy to this groove,*
speaks her movement:
>   *experience me . . . .*

The Sum Total
for August Wilson

Imagine this—
His declarative statement
of power and resistance
to our twentieth-century
racial nightmare.

His courage to deliver
REVOLUTION,
articulate
undeniably profound.

The documenting of
Black resonance,
realism diagnosed in
Ma Rainey's tradition.
Courage emanating
in a supernaturally
unbridled tongue.

Scripted offerings
essentially relevant to
un-deferrable dreams,
with insight into
the psychological struggles

of the Brothahood.

His spectrum of street music
bordered by conflicting fences,
and the agitation of toiled ambition
within our cultural song.

Examine the diagnosis:
The sum total of Black culture, he said,
and its difference from White America.[4]

Daily rituals of our
collective lives—
magnified, we
accepted out of necessity.
The many moods of
lost souls versus
the conscious griot;
revolutionary in mindset, yet
impoverished in surroundings.

Charismatic roots
dug up in the South and
laid to rest in Pittsburgh.
The tragedy of
historical division

---

[4] Bigsby, Christopher. *The Cambridge Companion to August Wilson.* Cambridge University Press, 2007.

sourced by the
dominance of a
violent America
intolerant to the
vibrancy of color,
the Colored.

1979
the documentation
began. His energy
delivered a magnitude of text
throughout a quarter
of a century.

This canon, the totem
of sorrow and rejoicing
amongst ritualistic
Black life,
has been mounted
as a landmark for
our world to witness—

An epic
literary
pillar.

Old Fashion Girl

for Markeya

Old fashion girl,
digs them righteous brothas.
The passionate lovers
who stand with big hands
to hold big hips,
kissing big lips,
rings of love seal partnerships.

That girl, she's old-fashion.
She conceives dreams through passion
and breathes life into the vision.
With precision
it's the rhythm that keeps her in tune.
Lyrics and melodies swell within the comfort of her
womb,
and as her belly grows round, full like the moon
her confidence knows it's not a moment too soon

because old fashion girls expect the unexpected.
Mama holds it down when things are getting hectic.
Never mind what you're doing,
Sis' got it together
and you won't forget her smile
that radiates ever, like the sun.

She's warm, and the girl loves to laugh,
drinking silly-girl juice from a champagne glass.
Old fashion girls, they've got a lot of class.
You wish you had the charm an old fashion girl has.

Now, old fashion girls,
they do love the Lord.
Walking quick and steadfast,
they live by the sword.
This woman personifies compassion and virtue,
but don't cross ole girl
'cause you know she will hurt you!

Keeping family together when the storm passes through
and shares the peace that keeps your spirit anew.
Inspires young girls to believe that whatever they do
that Old Fashion Girl essence dwells deep within you.

Lamiah

On a beautiful
SHINING day in May we prayed
and welcomed her in.

BFFs

for Juju

Mistaken mad dash
in the middle of Paris
brings lifelong laughter.

A Haiku in Three Acts

for Julia Pace Mitchell

Hills above the hood,
kick-ball-change across The Yard
into Broadway soaps.

The NJOB Experience

Perched on the edge of his amp,
he thumps'n'slaps a funky line
laying down a hard bass rhyme.
It matures where he sits.
The *riddims* nurtured
through painstaking concentration,
booming physical grooves
making that thang move!

Deliberate strokes are arranged.
They arouse what you sense in your soul—
an oscillating dimension
within random signatures of suspended time.
You'd expect exhaustion after one tune.
That's just how potent his force is
the moment he turns the bass up.
Invigored stamina propels this
commanding desperado
on bass *gui-tar*...
His music is his business, and
You can't get to the top
without the bottom!

Deep-toned blues
are fertile enough

to trickle and ooze
through fingertips meshed with string.
He bites that bottom lip
when it gets real good.
Every change calculated by a timed caress.
Right arm on top, the left cradles the bass to his chest.
With affection, it contracts to release each chord.
On a sunburst of quarter notes,
he bounces up and down
like a marionette without strings—
head leaned back,
eyes pinched shut,
hips swivel
to the thump,
crowd movin' with the hump.

Bliss in the pocket with reckless control,
hip-hop-laced jazz,
house, rock 'n' roll.
His centerstage ego is showmanship,
pulsating smooth punctuations in each move.
He finds the edge of his tune
and does a high-skilled balancing act,
like a fingertip acrobat,
before diving head first
or free-falling with ease
into this vortex
of sound.

Dangerfield

Suited and booted,
Detroit classical trumpet
delights the bandstand.

Azola Gypsy

Your fingers tap dance
across four strings as if it's
me you serenade--

Conga Beauty

Her circumference
mirrors the curves of his con-
ga: voluptuous.

dance floor conversation remix

(...i wanna rock...i wanna rock...i wanna rock...i wanna rock...)[5]

bruh: dag, gurl! you fine.
i love how you move.
you ain't married yet????
i'm feelin' this groove.
my spirit deeply feels
the need to explore
our possibilities
beyond this dance floor.

(...don't stop... get it, get it! Don't stop... get it, get it!)

sis: word, brotha?
is that a fact?
we groovin'...! and
you focused on of allathat?
and how deep in your spirit
do you feel that need?
I might be that magic
you lacking, indeed!

---

[5] Luke featuring The 2 Live Crew. *I Wanna Rock*. Atlantic Records, 1992. CD.

Lonesome

Wear sunshades to hide
sad eyes if you want your al-
ibi kept quiet.

Here We Are

here we are,
thirty-year-old schoolgirls.
we're girls who swoon at love.
chasing it like quixote's windmill.
daydreaming whimsy
while despising
every part of the game there is.
conjuring up careers
with demands we'd sacrifice
for sincere fidelity securing our legacy
of bright-eyed, beautiful seeds we protect.
a companionship with delicious sex
and, even better,
sharing partner-prepared meals,
playlists and road trips,
the occasional lazy morning, or crazy late midnight.
zones of simple comforts too often
not quite within reach.

and why?
because, for now,
we come home alone,
indefinitely.

here we are,
thirty-two, thirty-five, thirty-eight years old,
not feeling old,
not BEING old.
but feeling and being old enough to build a life
with that *one* of great significance.
independence is championed, self-sufficiency esteemed.
but the truest, sometimes loudest, sometimes quietest
desire
is to be dependent on that shatterproof bond
we somewhat foolishly still believe in,
and why shouldn't we?

here we are,
forty, forty-four,
fifty-two years old,
making decisions we don't want to make
because of experiences we never thought we'd have.
and why?
because we don't want to settle.
though the politics of "settling"
have been overanalyzed and less understood,
the gamut of unsettled experience
is here.

we never dreamed it would be this way.
didn't prepare for this to unfold.
it's just not what we thought.
while forever empowered by not *needing* a man,

this wasn't the plan.
but often that is who we are, who we become.
existing in dimensions that do little
to represent our full extent.
(even *this* is not our proper context.)
we wonder why it's yet to manifest.
we ask ourselves, in quiet times,
time and time again,
even if we ask no one else.

here we are, still,
though we hold the vision in our minds.
resolute in our longings for
the cliché, the fairytale, the dream...
an enviable love.
a connection.
the hashtag: team.
the imperfection of lives molded together,
the main ingredient of commitment and time.
the ups and downs
the joy of growing pains,
the ugly struggles
and the humble wins therein.

even when
we see countless loved ones and friends
and folks we don't know,
and ourselves
fall victim to

marriages that crumble
under the strain of pained life,
we're still waiting for our turn
to get it right.
or get it wrong and move on.
but, to finally get into it.

and so we wait.

we work. we date. we don't.
we leave the country. we adopt new cities. we go back to
school.
we change
our jobs. our hair, our bodies.
we go to the gym, then to the club, then to church. or to
temple.
or to mosque. or to therapy.
and everywhere else.
we creep, we have babies. raise families.
get jaded. self-preserve.
we do the things we want to do. and things we don't.
we purchase our homes and buy our own fine jewels.
we nurse ourselves back to health,
take trips,
accumulating passport stamps,
together, or alone,
cosigning on shared experiences
we wish weren't so common.
we persevere and carry on and

do what all the single ladies do.
what people outside of romantic relationship do.

or,
we just live each day
waiting to see how the dream unfolds.
ardent hopemongers, are we.
romanticizing for the sake of sanity.
or at least entertainment. we relish our girl talks
with degrees of expectation having more weight than
degrees from universities.
with determination
we live. outside of the dream.
or remix and reclaim it altogether.

some, longing for love,
learn to enjoy the journey,
come what may.
acknowledging,
sometimes ignoring,
the lonesome and confusing moments.
accepting illusions of love when they flutter by
in the grandeur of strong, handsome "maybes"—

we question if there's a future,
if even for a short time.
when it dissipates,
fuel for venting and never-ending girl talks,
shade thrown and shots fired,

and the truth comes out
>that the grass isn't always greener
>with a husband keeping years of junk in your yard,
>that family life is oft times more pain
>than champagne,
>that the solitude and autonomy
>and carefree weekends,
>and mornings to sleep in,
>all that *is life* to you exists not
>in their reality,
>that wives get lonely too,

we still wonder when our own "this is us"
will be scheduled for primetime.

through it all,
we either do, or do not, lose faith
as we wonder if it will show up, again—
and, this time, for good.

for others,
the journey is not so sweet
because the thought that something
—someone—
is missing
completely over-
or under-
whelms.

nevertheless,
we're here.

yeah. we are here.
as we
thrive.

Third Date Assertiveness
(A Poem on Straight To The Point Dating)

It goes without saying,
so, I'll just say it:
I'm not simply
                casually
        fond
of you.
                I see the potential for
                building something great
between us,
and envision
                        you&I
growing into something solid.
So, even though
you
        are
                single,
                or you
        say
you are,
I have two questions for you:

        Who is in love with you right now?
and;
        Who are you in love with?

Eggs: A Love Poem
for DAN

I.
When my grandmother would
make potato salad for the family
during holidays,
she'd put a small eggless batch
to the side just for me.
Her second to the last grand baby
did not like eggs.
Actually hated them.
But I would relish the love
in her eggless potato salad.

As a rule, I don't do eggs.
All of my life
I've been known
to pick them out of fried rice.
I avoid them for breakfast.
If a plate is prepared for me
and the gracious host includes
a serving of eggs *du jour*,
I'll discard the egg with the plate
when I'm done feasting, along with any morsel
that had the misfortune to mix with the scrambled.

Not to mention a time
I tried to eat deviled eggs at a house party
only to regurgitate the entire mayonnaise-y mouthful
in front of friends after the first bite.

This is my history with eggs.

II.
I have attracted incredibly beautiful men
into my life. I've had the greatest
love affairs, albeit mostly short-lived.
The endearment and respect, never lost.
None of them have ever
inspired an engagement
with eggs.

Something in my chemistry changed
when you came along.
My tolerance for the long-loathed,
intolerable egg grew into an all out,
unexplainable appreciation and willingness
to give them an experimental go.
Some strange phenomenon of accepting eggs
as a way of fully loving you.

I create recipes for scrambling them,
always with garlic and red onions, fresh basil.
As my beloved taste-tester, you delight in each bite.

You teach me the art of the omelet.
I beat you at your speciality,
though it is never a competition.
So many palatable ingredients in my omelet,
each a scrumptious and quirky detail
I taste in you. The deeper the love we share,
the more inspired my loving egg recipes.

You are amazed when I attempt
the most eggy dish I can muster: a quiche.
Preparing one from scratch is a labor of love.
So many ingredients are layered on top of one another
within the custard to make it work, and worthwhile.

III.
To start, an uninspired pastry dough,
store bought pie crust must do.
However, within that lucky crust is a bottom layer
of cream cheese, spinach and artichoke,
smoothed over with parmesan asiago shavings.
On top of the cheese, I pour out aged affection layered
with fondness and a variety of thinly sliced inside jokes.
I sprinkle a bit of intimacy with grated passion
and sharp sensuality mixed in.
Next is a generous helping of pre-mixed
tenderness and devotion
since they're always in season,
and taste so good when fully ripened.
As the crust begins to fill, I leave space for

sautéed onions, dill and capers
adding just the right smattering of flavor
to the custardy egg-filler once it is all poured in.

Topping the love-heavy pie off with a final touch
of turkey bacon, hardwood and smoked,
a porkless concession I make just for you,
I garnish the plate with a rich, creamy sauce of
forgiveness, compassion and understanding
once the quiche is out of the oven
and ready to be served.

The pleasure and satisfaction of
each delectable bite reminds me
of why I welcomed eggs, and you,
into my kitchen.

Other People's Husbands

My mother has a theory that most people marry other people's husbands... I finally have my own. ~Maya Angelou[6]

This was Mother's theory, so no need to question it.
God bless the child that's got her own,
this one that she fell for had caught her.
After being wedded to other people's husbands,
the Greek sailor before the South African revolutionary,
she had finally married her *own* husband in the Brit.

Seven years her junior,
blue-collar intellectual.
A creative with known proclivities for the bottle
and long-legged feminists.
Despite not caring much for the institution itself,
and being talked into matrimony for the third time
by her beloved Jimmy, Maya found
contentment and compatibility with this white man
she loved, who loved her even more. At peace
with the comfort and joy they shared.
Their attraction, strange to others,
built a home upon solid domesticity.

Nearly a decade later, she decided

---

[6] Hercules, Bob and Rita Coburn Whack, directors. *American Masters – Maya Angelou: And Still I Rise*, PBS, 2017, www.pbs.org/wnet/americanmasters/maya-angelou-film/7533/.

that this marriage with her own husband
need not interfere with the grand life of her own,
prior to and without him, she had built.
And to which, after him,
she remained married.

The Walking Nerve-Ending

I.

I have never met a stranger who did not intrigue. Paint a
face on a rock, and I'll smile and say hello.
Remembering to wave to the baby geese on the side of
the Meadowbrook, I delight in their annual springtime
arrival. I imagine that Mom and Pop Goose
acknowledge each time that I pass by and return a polite
goosey greeting of their own. Being born post-winter, as
I was, has a bearing on what enthusiasms I share over
the baby geese.

There's an innate reverence I have for life, no matter the
form. I cannot kill a bug. Nor will I appreciate it. But I
acknowledge that it is living. Some time ago I learned
that, though we celebrate the start of the new year in the
dead of winter, the more accurate timing would be in
early spring, with its awakenings of nature and new-
birth.

II.

Having a deeply-rooted fascination with the nature of
romance, I am an archaeologist of love. Countless hours,
I spend, digging up stories of tried-and-true committed

affairs of the heart. Well-worn love. Unbreakable and shatterproof. Fought for and slowly won. Or lost, yet restored by heroics and histrionics. Despite changes and children, the challenge of pre-existing conditions, dalliance and betrayal, or growing in and out of, then back into desire for one another. I am less interested these day (not altogether *dis-interested,* just less) in the fairytale of how people meet or decide to stand poised for temporary matrimony. I want to unearth the magic that compels decisions to stay in–or even more fascinating–return to unfailing love through the decades, and throughout many lifetimes, experiencing fulfillment while the complexities of love–bound to commitment– work themselves out.

III.
Asking a friend what he thinks I'm known for, he said my "openness" and "confidence." Commanding presence. I was groomed for leadership, though I've yet to take hold of any reigns. I create a game with myself trying to discern what I am missing in that unknown pane of my fourth Johari window. I am both risk-taker and high risk, high anxiety and zen. Palm trees and subways. Hood and neighborhood. Hopemonger with pragmatist tendencies. Increasingly more straight to the point and shoot from both hips, and less cat-got-your-tongue or beat around the bush. Attempting equanimity, though I fail. And while I fail, that is neither good nor

bad. I've had the good fortune to inherit great style with designer genes. A poet's mind with a minister's heart.

I am upbeat and downbeat. Hermit yet bon vivant. Storyteller and listener. More student than teacher. Decidedly 'Strong Black Woman' sometimes, embarrassingly 'weak and needy' at others, depending on the day of the month. PMS is real. Those days I steal away from the general public–and from my timeline– realizing that like waves, the nerves will swell up throughout and around me, then just like that, they settle. No audience is necessary while in process.

And I cry, oh boy, do I cry. When overjoyed and overwhelmed. At birth and at death. As I laugh and when deeply pained. Angry tears burn the most, but soothe when released. The catharsis of shed tears, both emotional and physiological, is a necessity for me. When there are no more tears, I think. And my thoughts become things. Pray. Meditate. Focus on faith. Everyday moving forward knowing that incremental progress is still progress.

It is a slow realization that my exposed nerve-endings and this tremendous vulnerability is not a flaw in personality nor something to diminish. I am often in the deep end, with my feelings, with my love and in walking through life.

It is in the deep end that one learns the tranquility of floating on top of the water, despite its depths. Despite what lies beneath. In the deep end, one learns to swim, or exercise the faith to trust God, then walk on water.

Let Them Love It
for Tshego

Parading a hodgepodge of mix-n-match first choices
and backups in front of your large closet mirror,
we cackle and carry on in the same ways that I do
with girlfriends back in the states.
Instant fashion shows determine what to pack,
whether in Brooklyn or Johannesburg.
Between sips of sparkling Villiera and uncontrollable
laughter,
we pick and choose our *lewks* to be just right
for upcoming nights in Cape Town.

You shimmy into a fitted asymmetrical pink'n'tan
number.
Clingy and feminine. Voluptuously flattering.
Patent leather tan pumps, pink Betty Boop bows
fastened onto the backs.
The look is almost perfection.
If not for the black leggings stretching from beneath
the bottom of your dress,
as if to redact sexy sensuality and strike it from the
record.
With modest rationale, you have your reasons:
Better to wreck the entire look
than for others to notice the abundance

of barely discernible ripples seen through the back of the dress.

"*Guurrrl*, cellulite!??"
I sip more fermented sparkles,
thinking over the many wonders
of a woman's body.

"....LET THEM LOVE IT!"

Sitcom

for Nikita

my life is a situational comedy when we're together:
you being shenanigan-prone,
me, the visceral voice of reason
(or vice versa, depending on the situation).

us, the encounterers of one dubious incident after
another—
(celebrity bar-fights in the hollywood hills,
haggling tambourines in tijuana,
heroic sunrise hikes in the canyons before
djembe-filled sunsets on venice beach.)

comedic timing so genuine
(marked by high drama and season cliff-hangers)
i wonder when we'll sign
a six-figure deal
for our award-winning
commitment to the script—

Hong Kong Disneyland

Chinese monks ride It's
A Small World After All, yet
snap photos of me.

Duck

I had no real interest in visiting Helsinki,
bottom of bucket list adventure.
But with twenty-two hours of layover,
I booked a seaside room
overlooking the Gulf of Finland.
This overnight stay would be much more
mellow than the night before.
Fourteen hours running
through Bangkok night markets,
swinging by a swingin' set at Smiles Jazz.
Craving midnight green curry,
2 AM Thai massage.
Quick nap before morning departure.
Direct flights not as preferred
as carpe diem.

Afternoon arrival
and I quickly learn that the Hong Kong dollar
is no match for the euro,
forcing conservative spending
if I am to make it back to New York
without breaking the piggy bank.

This prompts my first inclination
to skip the sandwich.

It is overpriced, I think.
Scanning the Flying Dutch menu,
(that small riverboat restaurant
downstream from where I managed
to stand up on a Baltic Sea paddle board
during a choppy-watered six minutes),
it sounds delicious enough:
Pulled Duck Confit Slider.

Surely delectable, this duck,
I almost pass for something
more run-of-the-mill
and average priced
and American,
like chicken fingers and French fries.
I don't even know if this is on the menu.

But, I decide to give it a chance,
count my euro then buy the slider.

Several years later,
there are days when I daydream
of that little hero.
I envision our meeting
all over again.
How does pulled duck
change one's life?
The tender treasure found
within such a tiny sandwich

piled high with spiced fowl.

I will visit Helsinki again.
If only to re-experience
the culinary indulgence
of shredded succulence.

Forever For Her

She wasn't mine
but I hold her as dear
as if she were
Didn't grieve her then
but miss her now
with you
Will never know her laugh, her grin
but celebrate her
in my own way
I grab your nose, and love that nose
For her

Though it brings me joy,
the marvel you found in her
is the delight she found
in having you

To struggle with,
or resist her loss
is to champion her being,
having been
    been *here*,
    been here *with you*,
    with you just as you are
Just as you are because of her.

You are, because she was.
She is, because you are.
Forever
For her.

Grand Central to Bronxville, Metro North

Steady, steady, steady
the house-beat never fades.
In time, the train
evolves across its track
of ever-last. Motion
pervades meditation.

Steady, forward,
eyelids are heavy,
psyche entranced by the lull
of city passing
on rotating canvas.
I fight the urge
of surrendering to
unconsciousness
inside the subconscious
of four on the floor,
on four,
on four,
on four on the floor,

for fear of waking up
in Scarsdale…

Steady, steady, steady

in time. The train
evolves across its track
of ever-last.

Wedding Poem

Let's pretend your journey here
never quite began.
Pretend he never saw you, thinking:
man, she's kinda fly!
Pretend she wasn't digging
this cute, artsy new guy.
Pretend you both didn't feel that spark
when you truly looked in each other's eyes.
Pretend that the total vibe wasn't a complete surprise.

Imagine if one of you had decided to keep it moving.
Decided to leave your meeting point
simply at–*hello*...
Decided to pass on the slim chance
that maybe this chance wasn't slim at all,
but the onset of your opportunity
to welcome love for the long haul.

Imagine if you'd never resolved
that the two of you would get it right!
Or if you allowed certain obstacles
to eclipse lifelong delight.
You didn't get hung up on any differences,
but wrapped your arms around the sameness.
Tossing aside any preconceived plans

you found the mutual to embrace,
then placed in the palm of your hands.

You found infatuation and ran with it,
grabbed affection and danced with it,
uncovered enchantment and basked in it,
stirred up amusement and laughed with it.
Aroused passion and sang with it,
discovered joy and welcomed it,
captured adoration and cuddled it,
exposed vulnerability, found comfort in it.
Took undeniable chemistry, generating new life
to establish this journey, together,
now as husband-and-wife.

heartbreaker

at some point you'll hear:
I just can't do love right now.
who will be speaking?

I Pray This Means Farewell, Wretched PMS!

Fair menses—
you have shown thy face,
and in thy grace i pray thee,
wash away the glooms
of yesterday that
the morrow may fully
cheer me.

Amen.

Detox (a mantra)

Detoxify yourself, dear love,
    from illusions of love detox.

From the contusion that love unrequited may bring,
    sleep until spring, if you must.

That times were good, you should soon forget,
    for remembering leads to great sorrow.

That you soon may forget gives birth to new hope:
    might true love be discovered tomorrow?

And if not tomorrow, dear love, then please sleep,
    so that you may forego strong desire to weep.

And if you do weep, Dear Lord, may He cleanse
    your dependence on love through faulty, rose lens.

So, detoxify yourself, dear love,
    from the illusion of love detox.

Sweet muse, I beg thee, reveal unto me
    the remedy of romantic detox.

Mad Pianist @ Zinc: A Suite in Three Parts

I.

As he plays, you will sense an urge to:
a) give birth to something or someone
b) give up the ghost
c) prepare to dive out of an airplane
d) board a spaceship flying either toward
or away from the sun (or atop a surfboard high
or below a fierce ocean wave)
e) listen to a grand chorus of owls and rhinoceri
f) all of the above

And as he plays, you will know that:
a) sitting in the back of a dark bar in the village
does little to satisfy the moment
b) getting up to dance would be more fulfilling
than concocting absurd lists exploring the gravity
of the moment
c) you should probably pay attention to the piano solo
now
d) again, all of the above

II.

I spoke to a gentleman from Iceland at the end of the set
and the feeling was mutual. Through his broken English,
his eyes said it all:

"It's otherworldly, the way he plays."

And it is.

It's almost as if he were preparing for the Lord of Hosts,
himself, to pull up in a chariot, ablaze. It was as if he
were an angel, not one of those white, cupid-looking
cherub angel babies, but a splendid warrior, multiwinged
archangel, ranked high with cacophonous majesty! You
feel that he would score the battle of armageddon, a
symphony orchestra of the new earth dawning. He plays
with the invocation and authority of something
beyond—pianist. A confirmation of the realm of glory
outside of the physical and metaphysical and disbelief.

III.
witness him.
surely, he's insane.
i wonder if this is what genius looks like?
i wonder what his brain looks like on the inside?
i wonder what he sees as he pounds the keys?
i wonder how many breaths he takes to finesse the flow.
is it too blinding for his own sight, i wonder?
does his mental composing space,
if rendered on graph paper,
look mathematical?
chaos theory, perhaps?
full of differential equations of the highest musical
order?

are his fingers are on
performance enhancers? or speed? or ginseng? viagra?
i wonder if playing *this* is just as pulchritudinous
and powerful and haunting to him
as it is to me
listening?

A Train Local @ 2 AM, NYC

burlesque showstoppers
on the 2 AM train
from west 4th to far rock,
performing in full grandeur
with a full audience of themselves
(full of themselves)
they are stars, all of them,
qualifying the lyric
"it's raining men, hallelujah"
too old to be teens, too young to be grown,
swinging about the pole,
every vertical pole on the train
on cue
jutted hips
flailing arms, wrists limp
gucci-sneakered feet in the air
not doing what strap-hangers do, but
swinging
upside down from the rails
very *va! va! va! voom!*
and vivacious
sashaying up and down the aisle
of that last car of the train
moving at breakneck speed
through jolts of unsteadiness

sloppy execution of routines
all things drill team/cabaret/sensual and erotic
with silly *savoir faire*
marching about
like a drum major,
a different sort of drum major for justice,
like that one in the uniform with the high-
heeled boots, white mesh bottoms, purple briefs
white script across the cheeks,
and a mardi gras mask tilted on the side of his head,
whistle clenched between his teeth,
his lips brimming with proclamation
en concerte and surround sound:
.....*what'chall talkin' about..? mmmm.!. NUTHIN...!*
dropping to the meanest, and fiercest Chinese split
that would befit broadway's center stage.

you ain't seen new york city nightlife
'til you've been on the A train-local
from west 4th to far rockaway
at two'o'clock in the morning.

Untitled Poem of Intention (1999)

I.
Though I once shed everlasting tears of yesteryears
my vision remained crystal-clear and focused
while folks were calling bogus
'cause we let our dreams inspire
now we're making empires manifest
like I say nothing less than what I believe

'Cause I'm inspired by the ancestors like sista Eve
she was the first mother of dreams achieved
I'm talking – wife, poet and MC
completed beautifully
keeping one almond-set eye
on my kismet prize
while the other two are daring and staring you
in your affairs and one declares
this, right here, this is the time to shine

See one day you have to recognize and define
what, or rather, who, is seeing you through this
as the spirit leads the service
meditate on your purpose
beyond surface
it's only worth it when you're putting in hard work
for your little bit

So, I'm gonna commit
to flippin' these dreams in to reality
'cause you see that works for me, and my family
and keepin' this loc'd head to the sky
I give thanks because
my faith stays on the Most High!

II.
The way I see
it was always made for me
see, I was chosen
to rest in a predestined destiny
the quality of my life given was said
the moment my pop's seed reached the egg

Now, if you would've read
then you would've knew
the same thang applies to you
my words true
we all have business to tend to

See, when you
grab hold to your vision
keepin' faith in the One who's risen
elevatin' your mind
so you don't keep trippin' and dippin'
through these days in a haze
yeah, it might get a bit crazy

But, hey!
We're all about progression
up in this rhyme session
and there's no guessin' the Most High will keep blessin'
if you learn the lesson NOW!
So, go'n and get rid of that foul,
so we can see that beautiful smile, chile.
We all got work to do,
and I'm right here with you.

She'll Get a Prayer Through
for Momma

It's common knowledge amongst family and friends,
that if you need things to happen in your life,
whatever it is, no matter the size,
she'll get a prayer through for you.

As those in her circle well know,
that whatever you need God to move,
mountains, molehills, any problem in between,
she'll get a prayer through for you.

You're her firstborn or last,
a student in her class,
or just crossing paths for the moment,
ill with the sniffles, or a threat to your life,
she'll get a prayer through for you!

Now, perhaps decisions need to be made,
and the outcomes are weighing you down,
waiting on that job, a promotion or raise that is due,
she'll get a prayer through for you.

Say you need God to move that special someone
into -- or out of -- your life,
neighbor or co-worker, a love or a friend,

she'll get a prayer through for you!

This special woman has a direct connect
to our God, and is a prayer warrior VIP.
She'll go to Him on your behalf
and sincerely, for you, intercede.

An example to those who love and respect,
she affects any problem through prayer.
We learn to talk to the Lord,
believing through faith,
He'll give peace and replace our despair.

After so many years, we are returning the love
and extend our own prayer that's true:
*May He bless and keep you, all of your life,
and, we pray, God's Grace upon you.*

Haiku for June April

Personality
as big as her voice and heart.
June April was art.

Haiku for Anisa

stereo love songs
dipped in hip-hop soul grooves, grew
songbird Anisa.

Years After The Goodbye I Missed
for Cheryl "Shay Shay" Wells

Caught you in my dream—
The autumn goodbye I missed
was today's hello.

The Big Homie
for Marcus

I only have one.
Different sides of the same coin.
Wes*ssiiide* G's at heart.

The Years Between Us
for Daddy

if only we'd been born
without thirty in between,
we'd've been best friends.

Fancy Footwork

for Ms. Mai's Ajman Habibis

They vault across the field like it's a trampoline.
Football bouncing like hoop dreams.
They're almost elegant in the way they dive for it,
midair–
back arched, arms stretched to mimic motherland
choreography.
Each movement that raptures the ball
enraptures the boy.

Ever seen feet shimmy on a football field?
Does he hear: "It's time for the percolator!"
when he fakes left
through a chorus line of players?
Metatarsal metaphysical acrobatics,
even the fat ones are fancy with it.
Light on their feet, they trip the light fantastic
across their grand stage, driven to score.

They're tireless, those feet.
They crisscross in athletic musical time,
then suspend with dissonance for eons of seconds
while colliding, unbreakable, on the green.
Swiveling around the ball with speed,
they are forbidden to touch it with their hands.

Maintaining full steam, they manage, however,
to forward it toward the goal with everything else:
in between arches and ankles,
bounced off the top of a knee.
A calculated isolated chest movement
sends the ball to a mate's head,
who's panting in earnest, less than a step behind.
Is the goal even to score, at this point?

They are so masterful, completely reckless and free.
Adrenaline in the wind pushes them
forward, backwards, and even sideways.
That black and white ball has them all on a short leash.

In custom trainers and sportswear,
they are all experts in their own way.
Yet each one questions, then listens, then questions again
what the other has to say about the play.

The call and response of it all:

   --Yalla!!
        -- Agulak!?
   --Shoo???
        -- Aiwa!

The field teeters from side to side
by these indefatigables stampeding
such a lucky ball.

They respect it. They respect the field. And they respect
one another.
They sort themselves into teams, and gather around
to applaud great effort shown
whether the golden goal is made or not.
Their laughter hovers over the field and lingers in the
hot sky
when a kick sends the ball hurtling beyond the goal post
into eternity.

Once the game draws to a close, they plop down,
legs folded beneath them or laid out from exhaustion,
and give their feet well-deserved reprieve.
On AstroTurf within the manicured land,
surrounded by sand in the middle of the desert,
my habibis compete in their own personal
World Cup every single day.

Abdulla Majed (Abood)

Abood is a Bumper Robinson-looking bamma.

If they ever come to the Emirates
looking to cast the life story
of a New Jack Swing era
sitcom heart throb,
Abood got it,
hands down.

Complexion, camel caramel,
adolescent turtle candy–
he got that 'good hair'
by Black folk standards,
fine wisps of black waves
cut into a high top fade.

Everyday I see a swoon in his eyes.
As if it's Hillman, 1993,
and Bumper's Dorian craves the attention of his Lena.
Or better yet, if we were situated in a comedy
set in Bedford-Stuyvesant,
and I published a fly magazine called *Flavor*
where college-interns turned errand boys
are completely smitten by...
well, my flavor.

I mean
what else could he be daydreaming about when he
stares?
Always eager to share, or read,
answer questions, correct or absolutely wrong.
He's one of the few that will end up in college.

The other day he asked about the best
university in *Ah-meh-reeeka*,
how it compares to Cambridge or Oxford.
Meanwhile half the class can't even spell Cambridge,
let alone inquire about comparative rankings.
I'm impressed by the question.
I tell him he needs to step his game up;
Smart and lazy don't mix
when it comes to Oxford or the Ivies.

So, what *is* he staring at?
With all of his *Yes, Ms. Mai*'s and
You want me to help? Ms. Mai's and
How are you today? Ms. Mai's…? and
his devoted grin, nose open wide.

Mohammad Malala

Malala turned fourteen when we met. Emirati male, he is a true emo: dark complexion to go with his dark mood. Tightly coiled hair, broad nose. He loves Obama, Biggie and Tupac, and freestyles in class everyday. Has a notebook full of lyrics written in Arabic and English. He asks me questions about the Black church. An experience he has firsthand knowledge of from traveling the West with his father. He wants to move to Compton when he becomes of age. I say, not if you want to live a full life. Fully aware of how many GOATs of both music and sports hail from Compton, who knows what awaits there for *him*?

He has my back, though I never asked for it in the first place. There's sadness in his eyes every morning. I want to give him a hug, as a big sister. The one I never got to be. That I am female, though his teacher, means he will never get that hug. Mohammad is here to learn, when he's here. He wants to absorb all things urban, Western, *Black* American. His ears perk up when I mention anything distinctly "Black." He's desperate to identify as such, though fully Arab. He is one of the few Afro-Arabs I've come to meet while in the Gulf, but had no idea existed in this duality.

I don't know how many years he spent in the States, exploring Southern California. But it left an impression on him. A grand endowment of the Compton Unified School District left him with a solid foundation of basic elementary English and academic aptitude. Very few of the others have been so privileged. He would be my top student if he did all of the work. He's definitely my deepest, most poignant. I credit that hood cultivation of the mind to the masters: Pac, Big and Malcolm X, of whom he often speaks.

Mohammad Malala has the kind of future in which I'd hope he remembers to mention or "thank Ms. Mai" during an acceptance speech, for having helped mold and influence his greatest achievements.

The irony is that I have no idea if I actually *am* helping him academically in this class. With such low proficiency among the others, how do I nurture a rising star? Perhaps I'm not in his life to be of scholarly assistance. Yesterday, during lunch, he sat at my desk to confide, "Ms. Mai, my mother's family calls me '*nigga*,' and I don't like it."

I am certainly more than his English teacher.

Reminisce Haiku
for Carey

There are times, still, when
I think we'll cross paths with joy
and laugh. Reminisce.

Bearable Grief

I carry this grief, smothering and heavy, out of necessity.
I am forced to live it.
Move with its weight around my arms and legs.
Across my shoulders and chest.
Measured inhales in tandem with slow beating heart,
I exhale bearable grief.
It infuses the breath moving through my lungs.
Its grey shades my mind.
And its pervasiveness invades.
It is overwhelming and understood, this grief.

It is a souvenir of the most devastating kind.
Not the delightful souvenir you are glad to place on your
mantle,
a keepsake representing the best of times.
Nor is it a memorable memento.
No, this is a souvenir of deep-rooted longing
to return to a space where the intention was to remain.
To rejoin the comfort of companionship
that has ended too soon.

There is a certain gentleness I experience as I hold this
grief.
It holds me back.
Becoming the companion I crave,

I fall asleep with it clinging to me.
When I awaken, it bows next to me as I pray,
and meditates with me
on how we may eventually part ways.
Very respectful it is of grief to honor your faith.

When I second guess, over and over,
my part in its arrival
it is neither a waste of wondering,
nor a waste of time
for this grief.
As a friend, it listens and knows its place.
And though, in time, this grief will be a memory,
it sticks with me in this moment, invading yet
welcomed.

Bridge/Fire

If you must, connect;
when it's time to burn the bridge,
thank God for fire.

Cover Letter

Sometimes I apply for jobs
for which I am well-qualified
and, during the call to offer an interview,
I decline.

I'm not sure which type
of crazy this is.

When job search turns into poem,
you are far gone.
What fated career path is this??
Between two Masters,
the pen and the dollar,
are degrees from institutions
with tuition that a poet
will never repay.

The tortured search for a job
for a poet, therefore, continues.

What vocation, then, brings satisfaction?
Satisfaction in finding just the right word
to form the pure thought
that will complete the sentence
of a poem (rewritten how many times?),

supersedes a perfect cover letter.

There is no cover letter
for a poem.

Poem for My Locs

Locs
freshly washed
lightly oiled
palm rolled
growing ombre
rooted strong
decades long
feeling light
soon
cut.

The Joiner

I refuse
to recluse.

A mantra repeated to self when
the excuse to remain tightly wrapped
within my own mindspace persists.
I'm no joiner, and it bothers me.
To no end. Because I know that
in joining, I'd likely be so much further
in the things I set out to do.
The habit of not joining is crippling,
yet is gratifying. It's what I know.

I social, though.
I social media.
I social calendar.
I rsvp and attend.
I social butterfly.
I social anxiety.
I AM social.
But join, I do not.

I've not joined
all of my life.
Excelled in not joining.

Revel in the irrelevance
of not joining.

Tell myself, feeling the urge:
>   *I will show up. Be relevant.*
>   *This will be a good place to join.*
>   *This is the time.*
>   *Become a part of this group.*
>   *The whole.*
>   *The team.*
>   *The community.*
>   *They need someone like you to join.*
>   *Go on.*
>   *Get involved!*
>   *Leave your mark on the world!*
>   *There is something here for you*
>   *if you join.*

Then I return to my own comfort. And I do not join.
Social hermit tendencies.

Yet, with intention,
I refuse to recluse.

Back Home

Growing up, my father would reminisce,
when you heard a brotha say
"down home" you knew he meant
down South.
If the brotha said, "back home"
you knew he was talking about Africa.
I thought about this during my
six hour flight
from Dubai to Kigali,
my first ever to the Motherland.
His words echoed:
down home, back home…
down home…South,
back home…Africa.

"Down home" carried a lesser weight
of unfamiliarity and romanticized perception.
Being a second generation Californian
with infrequent visits to the South,
I had been to the country a handful of times.
And Southern sensibilities coursed through
the veins of my great-grandmother America,
whose name had been chosen
to signify the only home in Texas
her mother knew.

But according to my father,
I was going "back home."
A home he had never seen for himself.
Nor any of my family, for that matter.
A continental home,
theoretical and ancestral,
attached solely by the bridge
of learned history and misremembering.

A bridge
built on the structure of tragic facts
and the inability to return.
Forced to endure and toil and reimagine
what home would become.

Generations later,
across this passage of history and knowledge,
on my own terms, I was coming
back home.

I AM :: MAI (Names & Meanings)
for anyone who has given much thought into what they will be called

Maisha (noun): Swahili translation of the word *life*, or to be "alive and well."

There was never a time that I didn't know this. Early in life, my parents made sure that I had a sound understanding of my given name. Spiritually-driven in her decision, my mother chose a name that meant "life" because of the new life promised in Christ's salvation and redemptive love, having returned to the church shortly before I was born. But, in that, I've had a less than clear etymological understanding of my middle name, *Kiana*. For as long as I can remember, my mother always insisted that the meaning was "delicate." Said that her inspiration for naming me *Kiana* came from a soft, delicate fabric called "Qiana" she once saw in a store. But, for years, I wanted a deeper understanding of the etymology of *Kiana*, the way that I did for *Maisha*. So I'd look it up to see what it represented in different cultures. In Irish, for example, *Kiana* means "ancient." In Hawaiian, it means "Moon goddess." I've read that similarly in Hindu, it means "divine or heavenly." *Kiana* also happens to be a Persian name, meaning "essence.

Then, one evening several years ago, a fellow globe-trotter and I sat talking about everything and nothing. The types of conversations that bring great enlightenment. He seemed to have another dimension of insight into my middle name. If you break the name *Kiana* into a compound of the two words 'KI' and 'ANA', this is what you get: *KI* is a Japanese variation of the Chinese word 'Qi' which is known as "*life* energy, *life* force, or vital energy flow." This encompasses the qualities of breath and air (or wind), which are essential to live. Qi IS life force. I've read that Qi is, in fact, the underlying principle in both Chinese martial arts, as well as traditional medicine.

With this lightbulb insight into the first syllable of my middle name, I went digging around to see what the second part was all about. I uncovered that *ANA* is of Hebrew origin and means "favor" and "grace." Some variations were "full of grace" and "mercy." That made sense in the grand scheme of how my life favorably unfolds year in and year out. If there is one constant state of my existence, it's that I lead a full life overflowing with the favor and grace of God Almighty, for which I am thankful. I live by the words of the Psalm, "Surely goodness and mercy shall follow me all the days of my life," and know this to be my truth. But I had no idea that a portion of my middle name literally contained the elements "goodness" and "mercy."

Our given names hold such significant value to a person's identity. The right name shapes one's calling and life work. Whether intentional, or unintentional, your name influences who you become. I appreciate my parents' foresight by gifting me with such a generous name. *Maisha Kiana*: LIFE full of favor and grace!

Like many names, *Maisha* became the playful nickname Mai-Mai, for short. The older I got, the more I liked the name *Mai* because it seemed so distinct. There are tons of Maishas and Mieshas and Myeshas and Maieshas that were born in the Seventies, particularly in L.A. I even share the name with a beloved cousin! Then in January of 1996, my senior year of high school, the UPN Network premiered a show called *MOESHA* starring R&B singer Brandy. I remember a tipping point once the show took off when people went from calling me *Maisha* to calling me *Moesha*. Not necessarily friends or people in my circle, but others who have a penchant for misreading or mispronouncing names. They would see: *Mai*sha, but think *Moe*sha. Or at times, others would see *Maisha* and think of the word "May" like the month, calling me "May-sha," which was, quite frankly, equally annoying. It's one thing to constantly remind people of how to spell your name; it's kind of expected when there are variations of the spelling. Although, my biggest personal pet-peeve is to misspell my name! But how draining it is to explain pronunciation of what I consider a very simple, and common three-syllable name. It's really not complicated, especially considering all of the creative and culturally distinct names that exist around us.

At some point, I cut out all extra explanations about pronunciation and spelling. How many times can you say, "Yeah, no. There's no 'e' in my name… nope, no 'y' either." Countless. So, eventually, I was introducing myself to everyone as *Mai*! I liked that it was short like a punctuation. And that you just didn't come across too many sistas named *Mai*. I liked that you could find tasty *Mai* Tais on the cocktail menu. I liked that *Mai* was already endearing to the friends who knew me best. It fit my peculiar personality. I liked the corny jokes people would make when they heard my name is *Mai*. "*Mai*?? Like miiiiiinnneee???" I chuckled at that way more than I ever did at being called Moesha.

Mai turned into "FlyMai" courtesy of my homeboy DJ A-Ski who came up with the ill moniker one night while partying in L.A. Then FlyMai became "Mighty Mai," a nickname given to me by my good friend, Tamir, uptown in Harlem. And this is how *Mai* came to be the name I use most often these days.

It wasn't until I moved outside of Dubai that I realized an Arabic dialect translation of the word WATER is "mai." *Wen al mai*? I was told means, "Where is the water?" Living in the UAE I would hear this at times when someone was thirsty and looking for a drink of water, given the water beverage company called Mai Dubai. (I loved driving past the Mai building at night and seeing my name all lit up!)

At the time, there was also an Arab comedian who had a joke that asked in the most annoying voice, *Wen al maaaiiiiiii????* My students, 10th grade Emirati boys, one day showed me the video on YouTube and (to my chagrin) found it hilarious to scream this out loudly in class. I quickly learned that if I was ever going to circle back to the lesson, I'd have to laugh with them.

I am fascinated that *mai* means water. Tying it back into my full name meaning, you cannot live, survive, or function without WATER. It is a necessity in leading a full, healthy LIFE. I'm always reminding myself to drink more water, and years later find myself chuckling in a funny voice, "Wen al maiiii??" when looking for my bottle.

Then there's the fact that I've always loved being near the water. I've been swimming since I was a toddler and now have a constant need to be near water, whether pools, rivers, oceans, hot tub jacuzzis...! In California, I'd visit the beaches of Venice and Santa Monica regularly growing up. One year after college, I taught art at an elementary school in San Pedro and would take lunch breaks at a nearby beach as well. I keep a mental snapshot of the view of the ocean from Pacific Coast Highway in Malibu which looks amazingly similar to the Camps Bay coast in Cape Town, South Africa. While there, I found myself wondering, "Does Africa look like California!? Or does California look like Africa!?" I'm also obsessed with peering out of the airplane window into the Pacific Ocean as it banks left after takeoff from LAX above the south beaches.

When I moved to New York, I'd take evening walks

on the Hudson up in Harlem, or would lunch on the waterfront at World Financial Center in Battery Park City. Showing up to interview for a teaching position at Kingsborough Community College, as soon as the bus dropped me off at Manhattan Beach, I already knew that I would get the job! It only made sense considering my relationship with water and beaches. Traveling to the Brooklyn beach campus each week was more than I could ask for. And during the few years I taught at the college, I held many writing classes outside by the shore.

I am made for being in close proximity to water. I love swimming in the ocean and turn into a bit of mermaid when in the flow of the waves. Visiting the Canadian side of the great Niagara Falls one spring midnight, the sheer volume of water was completely mesmerizing and haunting. I felt an overwhelming urge to get into the fierce, rushing water if only for a few moments. Of course it struck me that I would never return... But the majesty of the Canadian Falls! I was hypnotized. So I just stood enthralled by the sensory overload found in the cascade until it was time to go. Not to mention the year I spent in a beachfront apartment in the Emirate of Ajman experiencing the kind of life I've always known existed for me. A day at the beach...everyday!

The older I get, the more I feel like the *Mai* that I am. Decidedly. Energetically. Synergetically. I am *Mai*. I've fully shaped her identity and curated her image in ways that I'm not sure I ever did for *Maisha*. Of course,

I'll always be *Maisha* to the loved ones who care for and nurtured her. In some instances, when I hear someone say my full name, I feel like the 16-year-old who hasn't even begun to experience the fullness of life quite yet. The type of life that her name actually represents.

In choosing to go by Mai, there's also this strong sense of self-identifying, which I embrace as a way of life, more and more. No matter how intentional the givers of your name were in deciding what you would be called at birth, there's something empowering and fulfilling about deciding *for yourself* what people will call you. My grandmother knew that when she changed her given name as a Southern woman from Arkansas who would eventually settle with her husband and children in the nurturing community of 1940s Watts, Los Angeles. My mother also knew it when she decided to change her given name as a blossoming teenager and asked her mother to escort her to the name-changing office. They each had their reasons for why they would prefer to self-identify by choosing a name for themselves.

I've always appreciated the many Black Americans who have chosen names for themselves while incorporating into their identity aspects of African history and culture. I'd often think about changing my surname to one that does not reflect the slave masters who enforced ownership over my ancestors, but I never seriously considered an alternative last name. Besides, I love my father too much to change my name before marriage. When I hear the name "Perkins" I think of him, and how well-respected and highly-esteemed of a man he is. When I look at records and the only photo of my ancestral great-grandmother, Fannie Perkins, who was born generations ago in North Carolina in 1808, it makes me even prouder to be *Perkins*. The connection to her is deeper than explanation.

But we, my mother and maternal grandmother, are women who *choose* our names. We are women who decide after much consideration *what* people will call us. We are also women who answer to multiple names. Each name we answer to represents how we are seen from the people who use that name. Those who call my mother by her given name, the one she did not choose for herself, don't think any less of her for choosing her own name. I understand that. And because I do, I appreciate that with such an intentionally meaningful and divinely-inspired name that she's given me, *Maisha*, she makes no qualms about my preference to go by *Mai*.

THANKS & GRATITUDE

I'm not sure how customary it is to thank, literally EVERYONE, but since this is the first published manuscript of my career, I have a LOT of people to thank... *Ahem! (((big grin)))*

To begin: I want to thank God, the Father, for favor, divine timing and alignment, Godwinks, synchronicity, and His sovereignty as illustrated in my life each day I awaken.

To my parents, Charles and Barbara Perkins, for their ongoing prayers, support, unwavering faith and, of course, the depths of their love; my one and only brother, Marcus, the funniest person I know, and has my back like no other; my brilliant and strong niece Markeya, and our little princess Lamiah: I hold tremendous love and gratitude in my heart for each of you.

To those who have consumed every word that I have written up to this point in my career, to the early readers of *The Walking Nerve-Ending* (your enthusiasm and encouragement have carried me forward over the last year), and to those who will savor every word in this collection: THANK YOU all for being YOU in my life. What is a writer without an audience?

There are cherished friends and close confidantes, sistafriends and brothers-from-another-mother, distinguished mentors and professors, former teachers and counselors, ministers, associates, and creative partners that I'd like to thank for nourishing my foundational growth. Where would I be without your wisdom, influence and substantive love? My gratitude is infinite, and the support you've shown is reciprocated.

To all the folks doing it for the culture, who inspire me daily throughout my social media timelines, whether I comment or not, please know that you pour into me by your examples of greatness, and I thank you. I SEE YOU!!! Releasing albums, going on tours, publishing works of the highest standard, hosting podcasts and internet shows, starring in film and television, winning prestigious awards and global fellowships, accepting senior executive positions, becoming CEOs and entrepreneurs, celebrating business anniversaries and wedding anniversaries, starting families, traveling all over the world, and rabble-rousing and organizing and agitating, speaking truth to power, combating white supremacy, upholding all manners of equality and equity, and holding court in every arena as thought leaders! I see you, my friends, everyday. YOU fuel my belief that ALL THINGS ARE POSSIBLE to those who diligently remain on their grind!

Thank you and much love always to my alma mater, Howard University – Fine Arts and the community at large (HU.... YOU KNOW!), or should I say "Wakanda University!" Thank you VONA/Voices of Our Nation Foundation for being the onramp toward my decision to pursue my MFA. Thank you to my Sarah Lawrence College community and the exceptional writers who walked the campus and sat in workshop with me; I stand in awe of your accomplishments and immense talent. Let me express gratitude to The New School and GPIA for further shaping the ways I think and move throughout the world. A lifelong thanks to Normandie Christian School, James A. Foshay Junior High School, Hamilton High School, Crenshaw Gifted Magnet, and Young Black Scholars for molding me and laying the foundation to my success as a young scholar coming up. In the words of the great Nina Simone and Donnie Hathaway: "To be young, gifted and Black! That's where it's at!" Lest I forget: thank you to my various church families and to those who regularly pray for me, I express my reverent appreciation. Thank you to City University of New York and all of the students who entrusted me with their goal to become better writers. Thank you to the founders and editors at *Pop Magazine*, *Shoppe Black*, and *Relevant Magazine* for distributing my written contributions to their readership. Thank you to the special gatekeepers who have been door-openers on my professional journey. Thank you to my various professional comrades and genuine friends on the daily grind; you all make having a day job pretty sweet. I also thank the hundreds of brilliant, hilarious children in my life! What a joy you are to me. (Shout out to my godkids, Tavi & Mia!)

Thank you to my extended family on the West Coast including all of Mommae and Daddy Albert's children: Aunt Dophene and Uncle Lee (who contributed generously to my vision to publish this book); Aunt Dorothy and Uncle Waymon; Aunt Angie and Uncle Chris; Uncle Al; Aunt Jessie and Uncle Walter; Aunt Mable and Uncle Milton; and Auntie Brenda. It's not lost on me how blessed I am to have, literally, all of my aunts and uncles still in my life. I also thank my cousins (blessings to each of your individual families): Renae, Anthony, Kathy, Traci, Darren, Kiesha, Kyla, Kashala, Kyle and Kevin. What a treat it will be when we're all together again to reminisce about Mommae's House! Thank you to Brandy Alexander (IG: @bleezy3000) for your artistic vision in designing the cover art for *The Walking Nerve-Ending*, and for the masterful painting of the cover. I can't wait to one day hang it in my writing office. Thank you to Cousin Debra for your love and support, and to other members of Daddy's family and their children. To my BFF, Julia Jenkins, Esq, I can't express how proud I am of you! You both inspire and crack me up to no end. To my Cali crew: Nikita, Khyle, the Grays, and the Dames, I really miss living in the same city as you all more than I let on. To my #professionalblackgirl CHS crew Farah Parker, Monica Scott, Dominique Uolla and Maisha Cannon, you girls are a special brand of Black Girl Magic and I thank you for being the illest sounding board and the never-ending group chat that gives me life. To Dr. LeConté Dill, thank you for being a lifelong partner in manifesting these visions, and being a motivating factor rooted in #DILLigence. Endless gratitude to those who love and support me here in New York City (particularly, the Dangerfields, the Browns – love you so much Melly!, the Roberts, Ms. Fannie Neblett, among *countless* favorite people of mine across the city), where I've chosen to put down roots and create a magical home. Thank you to those who I've met in my travels around the globe. It is a tremendous blessing to have loved ones and kindred spirits here in Brooklyn, plus in so many different cities and countries, that I can call on at <u>any</u> time.

If I didn't write a poem about you in this book, just keep rocking with me! There are a lot of volumes still gestating in my mind and heart. God has enabled me with a gift and vision, and I plan to take this gift of writing *much further* past this moment. Lastly, to Dionicio: thank you for insisting that I drive Uber while I jumpstart my career as an indie author. Without your relentless support of my cockamamie idea(s), I'm not sure I would have been brave enough to actually jump into that driver's seat and take these NYC bridges and tunnels by storm! Look out for *UberliciousNYC: The Memoir* up next!!!

BELIEVE it in, guys!!!!

Love, Mai!

ABOUT THE AUTHOR

As a Cali girl in a Bed-Stuy world, the writing of Maisha Kiana Perkins embodies global bon vivant flair. With several blogs under her belt, including *Uberlicious.nyc*, she is a contributing writer for the online publications *Pop-Mag.com* and *ShoppeBlack.us*. She has also written for *Relevant* and *Bust Magazine*. Completing a Masters of Fine Arts in Creative Writing from Sarah Lawrence College, Mai Perkins has taught writing courses at City University of New York's College of Staten Island and Kingsborough Community College. She has also led "Improvisational Poetry: Inspired by Music" workshops for The Amistad Center for Art & Culture (TAC) at the Wadsworth Atheneum Museum of Art in Hartford, CT. As an alum of VONA/Voices of Our Nation Arts Foundation, her work has been featured in several anthologies including *Dismantle*. In addition to studying writing at Sarah Lawrence, Perkins also completed her BFA at Howard University, and received her MA in International Affairs with a concentration in Media and Culture at The New School's Julien J. Studley Graduate Program in International Affairs. ...and she loves to dance!

THE WALKING NERVE-ENDING

Follow Mai Perkins

Twitter: @flymai
Instagram: @flymai16
Facebook: @flymai16
LinkedIn: Mai Perkins

Revisit the blogs of Mai Perkins

www.Uberlicious.nyc
www.MaiOnTheMove.com
www.ArchaeologistOfLove.blogspot.com
www.MaiPerkins.com

Made in the USA
Middletown, DE
20 September 2018